_____

To

_____

From

_____

Date

Standard
BIBLE STORYBOOK SERIES

BIBLE
BEGINNINGS

Retold by Carolyn Larsen

Standard®
PUBLISHING
Cincinnati, Ohio

Published by Standard Publishing, Cincinnati, Ohio
www.standardpub.com
Copyright © 2012 by Standard Publishing

Printed in: China

Project editors: Elaina Meyers, Dawn A. Medill, and Marcy Levering
Cover design: Dale Meyers

Illustrations from Standard Publishing's Classic Bible Art Collection

ISBN 978-0-7847-3523-7

Library of Congress Cataloging-in-Publication Data

Larsen, Carolyn, 1950-
  Bible beginnings / retold by Carolyn Larsen.
     p. cm.
  ISBN 978-0-7847-3523-7
1. Bible stories, English--O.T. Genesis. I. Title.
  BS551.3.L345 2012
  222'.1109505--dc23
                              2011051491

17 16 15 14 13 12   1 2 3 4 5 6 7 8 9

CREATION

The miracle of creation showed God's amazing power and creativity. It also showed how much He cares for people. He created a beautiful world for us to enjoy, whether you love mountains, oceans, or deserts. He made tiny hummingbirds and gigantic killer whales. He made delicate yellow flowers and huge redwood trees. God thought of everything, and He made something for everyone to enjoy . . . creation shows God's love!

The Creation *Genesis 1:1-25*

B efore there were people on the earth . . . before there were animals on the earth . . . before there was a sun or a moon . . . before there was even an earth, there was only emptiness, darkness, and silence. Then God spoke four simple words, "Let there be light," and the miracle of creation began. The earth and everything in it was made by God. He did it all in six days.

God began Day One of creation

by making light and darkness. He separated the light and dark from each other. He called the light *day* and the darkness *night*.

On Day Two of creation, God created waters above the earth in the heavens and water on the earth itself. Then He created the sky and put it between the waters of the heavens and the earth.

On Day Three, God moved the waters on the earth together and separated them from the dry land. He called the waters *seas* and the dry ground *land*. He filled the land with plants and trees that grow fruits with seeds—seeds that would make new plants. That way the plants would keep growing more plants and fill the earth with flowers, bushes, and trees.

On Day Four, God put a light in the nighttime sky. This light is the moon. He also put stars in the night sky. God put a brighter light in the daytime sky. This light is the sun.

Day Five saw the creation of fish and other life in the seas. From the tiniest little seahorse to the mammoth blue whale, God filled the waters with life. Day Five is also the day that God made birds that fly through the sky. These sea creatures and sky creatures have babies so there will always be life in the seas and in the sky.

On Day Six God made all kinds of animals that live on the earth. He made insects like mosquitoes and caterpillars. He made small animals such as squirrels and kittens. He made large animals such as elephants and giraffes. He made farm animals like cows and goats. God made all the animals to have babies so that the earth would always be filled with animals.

God looked at everything He had made. He was very happy with all of creation. He had made seas and dry land. He had filled the seas with things that swim and He had filled the land with animals and plants. He had made the sun and the moon. But God wasn't finished yet. There was one more special creation on Day Six. This one is God's masterpiece!

God Makes People   *Genesis 1:26–2:3*

F or six days God was busy creating things. He made the whole earth and everything in it. Each of His creations was amazing. But on the sixth day, God made His most incredible creation. He made the first man using just the dust of the earth. Adam was made in God's own image. That means that people could think, make choices, talk, and

care about things just as God does. "Adam," God said, "I want you to give names to each of the animals I have created." Adam named them all, "That is a butterfly. This one I will call hippopotamus." But, when the naming was finished, Adam was lonely. He had no other human to be friends with; no one to talk with. God saw that Adam was lonely, so He made Adam fall asleep. While Adam was sleeping, God took a rib from Adam's side. God used that rib to form another human. This human was different from Adam though. She was a woman. She was called Eve.

Adam and Eve were the first people on the earth. God told them to have babies and fill the earth with more people. He trusted them to govern the earth and take care of it. God made a beautiful garden in Eden for Adam and Eve to live in. "I have given you plants to eat and trees that grow fruit to enjoy. I also made plants for the animals to eat," God said. When God was finished with all this, the sixth day ended. God looked at everything He had made. It was all good. God was happy with everything. So, on the next day, the seventh day, God rested.

Sin Enters the World *Genesis 2:8–3:24*

God put wonderful plants in the Garden of Eden that grew sweet berries and other delicious fruit for Adam and Eve to eat. Four rivers supplied water for them to drink. Adam and Eve had everything they needed in the Garden of Eden. God gave them important work to do. Their job was to care for the garden and rule over the animals that lived there. God gave Adam and Eve one simple rule to obey. He said, "You can eat fruit from any of the trees in the garden. They are all here for you to enjoy. But you must not eat fruit from the tree in the center of the garden. If you eat from the tree which gives knowledge of good and evil, you will die."

The serpent was the sneakiest of all the creatures God made. One day he crept up to Eve and asked, "Did God really say that you can't eat *any* of the fruit in the garden?"

"Of course not," Eve replied. "We can eat whatever we want except for the fruit of the tree in the center of the garden. If we eat or touch that fruit, we will die."

"Oh, come on," the serpent said. "You won't really die. If you eat that fruit you will just become like God. You will actually know the difference between good and evil."

The serpent kept tempting Eve to try the fruit and it looked so juicy and delicious that finally she grabbed a piece and took a bite. Then Eve gave Adam some of it too. Right at the moment they ate the fruit both Adam and Eve knew they were naked so they quickly tied some leaves together to make clothes.

Later than night God came to meet the man and the woman in the garden. But Adam and Eve were ashamed because they had disobeyed God, so they hid from Him. When God asked Adam why he was hiding, Adam answered, "I was afraid because I am naked."

"Who told you that you were naked?" God asked. "Did you eat the fruit I commanded you not to eat?"

"I did. But Eve is the one who gave it to me," Adam answered.

"Yes, but the serpent tricked me into eating it," Eve said.

God was very sad that they had disobeyed Him, but He had to punish Adam and Eve. So God made Adam and Eve leave the beautiful Garden of Eden. He even stationed a flaming sword at the opening of the garden so Adam and Eve could never go back inside.

Cain and Abel *Genesis 4:1-16*

A fter being sent out of the Garden of Eden, Adam and Eve had two sons. Cain was the oldest and when he grew up he became a farmer. Abel was his younger brother and he became a shepherd when he grew up. Adam and Eve taught their sons to give offerings to God. So, at harvest time, Cain brought an offering of grain he grew on his

farm. He presented his offering to God. Abel brought the Lord a gift of one of the best lambs from his best flock of sheep. The Lord accepted Abel's offering but He rejected Cain's offering. Cain became very angry.

"What are you angry about, Cain?" God asked. "Your offering will be accepted if you do what is right. If you do not do what is right and have the wrong attitude, then watch out because sin is going to destroy you!"

Cain could not get over his anger. The more he thought about his offering being rejected the angrier he got. He became jealous that Abel's offering was accepted so his anger was directed at his brother. Cain came up with an evil plan. One afternoon he suggested, "Abel, let's go out to the field together." Abel went for a walk with his brother out to the field. While they were away from everyone else, Cain attacked his brother and killed him. He thought no one would know what he had done.

But later God asked Cain, "Where is your brother, Abel?"

"I don't know," Cain lied. "Do You expect me to keep track of him every minute?"

But God knew what Cain had done. "You killed your brother," God said. "His blood cries out to me from the ground where you left him. I must punish you for what you have done. This ground will no longer grow crops for you, no matter how hard you work," God said. "Also, I will make you leave this place you call home." For the rest of his life Cain would have no real place to call home.

"This punishment is too hard," Cain complained. "You are sending me away from my land and away from Your presence. Everyone who sees me will try to kill me!"

"No one will kill you," the Lord said. "I will severely punish anyone who does." Just to be sure, God put a mark on Cain to warn anyone who might try to hurt him. So Cain left God's presence and settled in another land.

Noah's Story

After Cain killed his brother, Adam and Eve had another son. They named him Seth. When Seth grew up, he had a son named Enosh. During Enosh's lifetime people began to pray to God. About seven generations later a man named Noah was born. By then many people had stopped praying to God. They stopped obeying God. In fact, they just didn't care about God at all. Of course, it made God sad because the people He had created no longer cared about Him. But Noah still cared about obeying God, and his story changed everything.

Noah Builds an Ark *Genesis 6*

A dam and Eve had children. Their children had children. Now, generations later, the population of the earth was growing very quickly. It seemed that the more people who lived on the earth, the more selfish and greedy people became. Of course, God noticed that people had become very self-centered. Each one thought only about himself and how things affected him. It made God sad to see how evil people had become. They were dishonest and they didn't care at all about living for God or pleasing Him. They even did things that hurt one another. You know that things must have gotten very bad because God began to feel sorry He had even made people. His heart was filled with sadness and pain. He knew that He had to do something to stop people's evil behavior. So God came up with a plan. It was a good plan but it would not be easy for His loving heart. He said, "I will wipe out all the people on the earth—everyone I have created. I will wipe animals and birds from the face of the earth too, because I am sorry I made them all." However, there was one man on the earth who pleased God. His name was Noah.

Noah obeyed God even though his friends and neighbors did not. God saw Noah's obedience. He saw that Noah taught his three sons, Shem, Ham, and Japheth, to obey God. So God said, "Noah, I'm tired of the violence and evil ways of my people. I have decided to destroy the people and the animals on the earth. I want to save you because you honor me. So build an ark, a big boat." God told Noah exactly how big to make this giant boat and exactly what kind of wood to use and how to build it. He gave him specific instructions. The ark would be 450 feet long, 75 feet wide, and 45 feet high! It would have an opening very near the top of the

boat. It would have one giant door on one side. God said to build three decks inside: one on the bottom, one in the middle, and one on top.

God planned to destroy the world and the people in it by sending a flood over all the earth. This flood would wipe everything God had made off the face of the earth. But Noah and his family would be safe inside the ark.

"I want you to bring inside the ark with you two of every kind of animal and bird that lives on the earth," God told Noah. God made a male and a female of each species of animal come to Noah. Monkeys, camels, rabbits, goats, eagles, sparrows—all the birds and animals that God had created went inside the ark and lived on the three decks Noah had built. "Bring food onto the ark for you and your family and for all the animals too," God said. Noah did everything that God told him to do.

The Rain Begins *Genesis 7:1–8:5*

Noah finished building the ark exactly as God told him to build it. It took Noah many years to build the ark, but he kept working. When it was finished and all the animals were safely inside, God said, "Noah, take your family and go inside the ark too." It was time for God's plan to go into action. God shut Noah, his family, and all the animals inside the ark and rain began to fall. There was a male and a female of every kind of animal in the ark along with Noah, his wife, their sons Shem, Ham, Japheth, and their sons' wives. Noah had stored lots of food for all the animals and for his family in the giant boat too. He didn't know how long they would be in the ark, but God knew.

Noah was 600 years old when it began to rain. It rained and rained. Rivers got so full that water began to spill over the banks. Giant puddles formed on the ground. Pretty soon the ground was completely covered with water. Soon there way no way to tell where the rivers or lakes had once been separated from the dry land. They may have been worried about when the rain was going to stop. God's plan continued and it kept right on raining. The floodwaters got deeper and deeper. Finally the water was as high as the tops of the trees. Inside the ark, Noah, his family, and all the animals were safe and dry. They could hear the rain falling outside. As the water got deeper and deeper, it lifted Noah's giant boat right off the ground and it began floating.

The rain kept falling steadily on the earth for 40 days and 40 nights. It didn't stop raining. Soon, even the tallest mountains were covered with 20 feet of water. The great ark floated higher and higher—higher than the tops of the mountains. Still Noah and everyone in the ark was safe. But outside the ark things were not so good. Everything on the earth was destroyed. Every single person living on the earth died in the flood. All of the animals—birds, sheep, goats, cows, dogs—all of them drowned. Trees, plants, flowers, and bushes—everything was destroyed, just as God said they would be. No one was left on the earth except Noah and his family.

After 40 days and 40 nights the rain stopped falling. But the floodwaters were so deep that the ark kept floating and floating. The waters covered the earth for 150 days.

God remembered Noah and He sent a strong wind to start blowing across the earth. It began drying up the floodwaters. The water went down and down until finally the ark came to rest on the top of a mountain called Ararat. But the floodwaters were still too deep for Noah to let the animals out of the boat. Noah and his family had been living in the ark for about eight months, but it still wasn't safe to come out. They couldn't live on the earth yet.

A Brand New Start *Genesis 8:6–9:17*

Noah's giant boat came to rest on the top of Mount Ararat when the floodwaters began going down. The water was still too deep for Noah and his family to come out, so they waited 40 days. Then Noah sent a raven out. It flew back and forth, looking for a place to land. After a while Noah sent a dove out of the ark. It flew around and around

but could not find a place to land so it came back to the ark. Noah waited a week and then sent the dove out again. It came back to the ark again, but this time it had an olive leaf in its beak! The water was going down! Noah sent the dove out once more a week later. This time it didn't even come back! It was still a couple of months later before God finally said, "Come out of the ark, Noah. Bring out your family and all the animals. It's time for the animals and birds to have babies and fill the earth with life once again." So Noah and his family came out of the ark and saw the brand new world that was left after the flood. The fresh air smelled good. The sunshine felt good. But there were no other people or animals on the earth. They had all died in the flood. The only people and animals now were the ones who had been inside the ark.

The first thing Noah did was build an altar and give a sacrifice to God. He thanked God for keeping him and his family safe from the flood. God was pleased with the sacrifice and He said, "I will never curse the ground again. Even though man is evil, I will not destroy the earth and all its creatures again. As long as the earth is here, there will be summer and winter and day and night."

"I bless you and your sons, Noah. I want you and your sons to have more children so the earth will be populated again. You will rule over the animals and I give you all the plants. I give you everything," God said.

Then God made a promise to Noah and his sons. "Never again will I cut off all life from the earth by a great flood. There will never again be a flood as big as this one. I promise," God said. "I will put a sign in the sky as a reminder of my promise. Each time I see this sign I will remember my promise to you." The sign God put in the sky was a rainbow! Noah knew that the rainbow was a reminder of God's promise with all the creatures on the earth. Noah and his family were ready for a brand new start.

THE TOWER OF BABEL

Noah lived another 350 years after the great flood. Noah's sons, Shem, Ham, and Japheth and their wives came off the ark and set up housekeeping. Each of them had many children after they left the ark. That was exactly what God had told them to do. Those children were the beginning of the human population on the earth after the great flood. The animals that were on the ark had babies when they came back on dry land too. The earth was once again filled with life, just as God intended. The people lived and worked and worshipped God. They moved around and lived in various places. One group of people who lived near a place called Shinar made a poor choice, though.

The Tallest Building in the World
Genesis 11:1-9

After the great flood, all of the people who lived in the world spoke the same language. People who lived in various places could get together and everyone could understand what everyone else said. They could make plans or talk about the new world they lived in. They could talk about the great flood that their ancestors survived and the big ark Noah had built. They could talk about anything!

Apparently that was fine with God until one group of men had an idea. "Let's make bricks and bake them in ovens. That will make them strong enough so we can use them to build buildings." Before this new idea, buildings were made of stone. These men wanted to make buildings that were made of bricks that stacked on top of each other and were held together with tar. Everyone thought this was a great idea so the men began making bricks and building the new city. They talked about their city as they worked. They planned what buildings they would make. As they were talking, someone had another idea. "Why don't we build a tower in our city that reaches all the way up into the heavens?" he said. "It will be

the tallest building ever." All the other men thought this was a great idea. "We will be famous for our tall building," someone said. "We will be so famous that no one will ever try to break us up or make us move to other cities. We will be powerful and will stay together here in our city because of our famous tower."

The men didn't ask God about their plan. Maybe they did not even care how He would feel about it. They should have known that God would not be happy about it. He did not like that the men were making plans of their own. God looked at the city and the very tall tower they were building. God was not happy with what He saw. "The problem is that these men all speak the same language, so nothing is impossible for them," God said. "They are building this tall tower now but next, they will be able to do anything they try." God knew He had to stop the men. He did not want them thinking they were more powerful than He is. God had a simple plan to stop the men. He made everyone begin speaking different languages. Men who one day could understand everything others said could not even talk to each other the next day. No one knew what anyone else was saying. Now they couldn't make plans. They couldn't even finish building their tall tower. Then God did just what the men had tried to prevent. He scattered them over all the earth. They all moved to different places. The place where the men had started building the tall tower was called Babel because God confused their language there. And the unfinished tower was called the Tower of Babel.

ABRAHAM'S STORY

About seven generations passed after the unfinished Tower of Babel was built. That was when God scattered people all over the world. He made the people speak different languages. Next, the story of God's people focused on the family of Terah. This was an important family. Terah had three sons: Abram, Nahor, and Haran. Haran was just a young man when he died. Haran had a son named Lot. Abram married a beautiful woman named Sarai. They wanted to have a family. Unfortunately, Sarai could not have any children. One day Terah decided to move to the land of Canaan. He took his grandson, Lot with him. He also took Abram and Sarai with him. They walked and walked. They got to the village of Haran. The little family stayed in Haran a long time. In fact, they never moved on to Canaan. Terah died while the family lived in Haran.

Abram's Big Move *Genesis 12*

After Terah died, God had a special message for Abram. God told him to pack up his family and move away from Haran. God didn't tell Abram where he was to go. He just told him to start traveling. God made a promise to Abram. He said, "I will make you the father of a great nation, Abram. I will bless you. You will be famous and you will be a real blessing to other people. All people on the earth will be blessed through you, Abram!"

Abram obeyed God and took his wife, Sarai, and his nephew, Lot, and left Haran. He also took his servants and all the animals he owned. They left Haran and walked through the land of Canaan. When they were close to a city called Shechem, they stopped and set up camp. Many people lived in that area, but God spoke to Abram again and said, "I am going to give this land to you and your children." Abram was very happy so he built an altar there to celebrate. Abram kept

traveling because there was a terrible famine in the land of Canaan. The famine made it very hard to find food. There was no famine in the country of Egypt though. That meant there was food there. So Abram kept going until his family reached Egypt. As they were crossing into that country, Abram suddenly thought of something. "Sarai," he said, "you are so beautiful that I'm worried about a problem we may have. I'm afraid that the Egyptians will see how beautiful you are and will want you for their own. Since you are my wife, they will kill me so they can have you. So let's tell them that you are my sister instead of my wife. Then we can be sure they won't kill me."

So, Sarai told everyone that Abram was her brother instead of her husband. Sure enough, when the Egyptians saw how beautiful she was they ran

to tell the Pharaoh. Of course, the Pharaoh wanted Sarai to become one of his wives. So Sarai went to live at his palace. Pharaoh gave Abram many wonderful, expensive presents in exchange for Sarai. He gave Abram sheep, cows, donkeys, and even servants.

But God knew what was going on. He knew that Sarai was Abram's wife and not his sister. He wasn't happy that Pharaoh had taken Abram's wife. God sent terrible plagues on Pharaoh's household. It wasn't long before Pharaoh figured out what had happened. "Why did you do this to me?" he asked Abram. "Why didn't you just tell me that Sarai was your wife? Take her and get out of here." In fact, Pharaoh sent an armed guard to lead them out of Egypt. Abram, Sarai, Lot, and all the servants were escorted out of the country.

Abram and Lot Go Separate Ways

Genesis 13

Abram rounded up his large herds of cattle. He gathered up his servants and all his possessions. Then Abram, Sarai, and Lot headed north out of Egypt. Lot was also very wealthy. He had large herds of cattle and sheep and many servants. They traveled to a place between Bethel and Ai. This was the place where Abram had previously built an altar to worship God. They stopped there and set up their tents. This area was very fertile with gardens and grasses for the animals to eat and rivers for them to drink from. But Abram and Lot's herds of cattle and

flocks of sheep living together meant there were too many animals in one place. There wasn't enough food and water to support both of their large herds. The men caring for the animals began to argue with each other. Abram's workers said, "Our master is more important. His animals should get the food and water." But Lot's workers thought that Abram's herds should go somewhere else so that Lot's animals could have the food

and water. Their arguing got worse and worse until they were arguing all the time. The herdsmen were all concerned about their animals having enough food and water.

Abram knew this arguing was not good so he went to talk with Lot. "This arguing has to stop," he said. "After all, we are related. We need to get along with each other. Here's my plan: You choose which piece of land you want to live on. Take whichever section you want. Then we will separate and I'll take my family and animals somewhere else. If you want to move to some other place, I will stay here. But if you want to stay here, then I will move. It's up to you."

Lot looked at the beautiful Jordan Valley. It had lots of grasses and water. It was as beautiful and fertile as the land of Egypt. It was the best land around. So Lot chose that land for himself and his animals. He moved his family, servants, animals, and tents near a city called Sodom. The people of Sodom were very wicked. They sinned against God by the way they lived. Lot knew it was the best land for his herds and flocks.

Abram stayed in the land of Canaan. God said to him, "Look around you. Look as far as your eye can see in every direction. I will give all of this land to you. It will belong to you and your children." God wasn't finished with His promises. He said, "I will give you children. You will have so many descendants that you won't even be able to count them. So go for a walk and see your new homeland." Abram did just that. Then he built an altar and worshipped God.

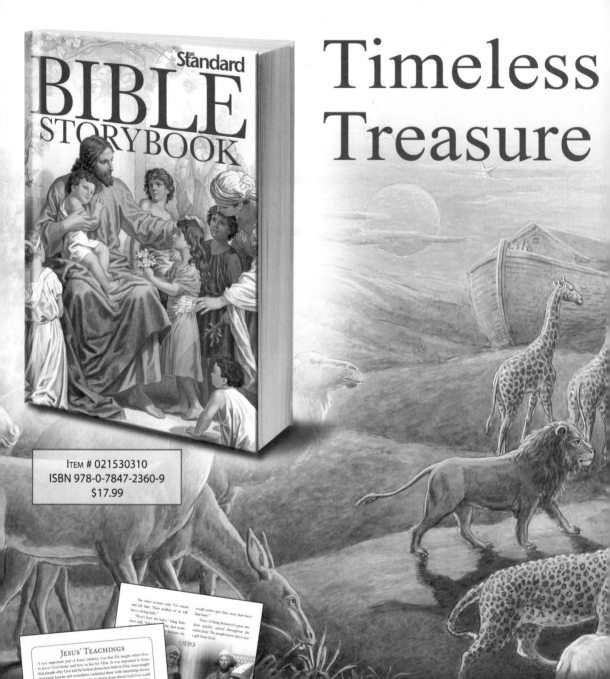

Timeless Treasure

ITEM # 021530310
ISBN 978-0-7847-2360-9
$17.99

The Bible is not 66 sections that have nothing to do with each other. Each book and each story builds on one another to give a complete picture of God's amazing love and grace. Each picture gives an understanding of the setting and culture of the biblical story. Share the story of God with your children through this wonderful book!

Standard ®
PUBLISHING
Bringing The Word to Life

To order, contact your local Christian supplier or **1-800-543-1353**
or **standardpub.com**